Appalachia

APPALACHIA

CHARLES WRIGHT

FARRAR STRAUS GIROUX

NEW YORK

Farrar, Straus and Giroux
19 Union Square West, New York 10003

Distributed in Canada by Douglas & McIntyre Ltd.
Printed in the United States of America
Designed by Cynthia Krupat
First edition, 1998

Library of Congress Cataloging-in-Publication Data
Wright, Charles, 1935-
    Appalachia / Charles Wright. — 1st ed.
    p.   cm.
    ISBN 0-374-10571-5 (alk. pbk.)
    I.   Title.
    PS3573.R52A66   1998
    811'.54 — dc21   98-16803

All the poems in Appalachia *have been previously published in
the following magazines:* Five Points, The Kenyon Review, The
Recorder, Poetry, The New Yorker, Virginia Quarterly Review,
Slate, Green Mountains Review, The New Republic, The
Carolina Quarterly, Field, The New England Review,
Sycamore, The Yale Review, The Nation, Thornwillow, The
Bitter Oleander, The Paris Review, The Oxford American, River
City, The Gettysburg Review, Excerpt, The Partisan Review,
The Ohio Review, Meridan.

In memory of my sister, Hildegarde Wright,

who lived there all her life

Contents

1

Stray Paragraphs in February, Year of the Rat, 3

Stray Paragraphs in April, Year of the Rat, 4

Basic Dialogue, 5

Star Turn, 7

A Bad Memory Makes You a Metaphysician, a Good One Makes You a Saint, 8

Thinking about the Poet Larry Levis One Afternoon in Late May, 9

In the Kingdom of the Past, the Brown-Eyed Man Is King, 10

Passing the Morning under the Serenissima, 11

Venetian Dog, 12

In the Valley of the Magra, 14

Returned to the Yaak Cabin, I Overhear an Old Greek Song, 15

Ars Poetica II, 16

Cicada Blue, 17

All Landscape Is Abstract, and Tends to Repeat Itself, 19

Opus Posthumous, 20

2

What Do You Write About, Where Do Your Ideas Come
    From?, 23

Quotations, 24

The Appalachian Book of the Dead II, 26

Indian Summer II, 27

Autumn's Sidereal, November's a Ball and Chain, 29

The Writing Life, 30

Reply to Wang Wei, 31

Giorgio Morandi and the Talking Eternity Blues, 33

Drone and Ostinato, 35

Ostinato and Drone, 36

"It's Turtles All the Way Down", 37

Half February, 38

Back Yard Boogie Woogie, 39

The Appalachian Book of the Dead III, 40

Opus Posthumous II, 41

3

Body Language, 45

"When You're Lost in Juarez, in the Rain, and It's Eastertime
    Too", 46

The Appalachian Book of the Dead IV, 47

Spring Storm, 49

Early Saturday Afternoon, Early Evening, 50

"The Holy Ghost Asketh for Us with Mourning and Weeping Unspeakable", 51

The Appalachian Book of the Dead V, 53

Star Turn II, 55

After Reading T'ao Ch'ing, I Wander Untethered Through the Short Grass, 56

Remembering Spello, Sitting Outside in Prampolini's Garden, 57

After Rereading Robert Graves, I Go Outside to Get My Head Together, 59

American Twilight, 60

The Appalachian Book of the Dead VI, 61

Landscape as Metaphor, Landscape as Fate and a Happy Life, 62

Opus Posthumous III, 64

Notes, 67

1

Stray Paragraphs in February, Year of the Rat

East of town, the countryside unwrinkles and smooths out
Unctuously toward the tidewater and gruff Atlantic.
A love of landscape's a true affection for regret, I've found,
Forever joined, forever apart,
                                        outside us yet ourselves.

Renunciation, it's hard to learn, is now our ecstasy.
However, if God were still around,
                                        he'd swallow our sighs in his nothingness.

The dregs of the absolute are slow sift in my blood,
Dead branches down after high winds, dead yard grass and
        undergrowth—
The sure accumulation of all that's not revealed
Rises like snow in my bare places,
                                        cross-whipped and openmouthed.

Our lives can't be lived in flames.
Our lives can't be lit like saints' hearts,
                                        seared between heaven and earth.

February, old head-turner, cut us some slack, grind of bone
On bone, such melancholy music.
Lift up that far corner of landscape,
                                        there, toward the west.
Let some of the deep light in, the arterial kind.

Only the dead can be born again, and then not much.
I wish I were a mole in the ground,

                         eyes that see in the dark.

Attentive without an object of attentiveness,
Unhappy without an object of unhappiness—
Desire in its highest form,

                dog prayer, diminishment . . .

If we were to walk for a hundred years, we could never take
One step toward heaven—

                you have to wait to be gathered.

Two cardinals, two blood clots,
Cast loose in the cold, invisible arteries of the air.
If they ever stop, the sky will stop.

Affliction's a gift, Simone Weil thought—
The world becomes more abundant in severest light.

April, old courtesan, high-styler of months, dampen our mouths.

The dense and moist and cold and dark come together here.

The soul is air, and it maintains us.

Basic Dialogue

The transformation of objects in space,
                              or objects in time,
To objects outside either, but tactile, still precise . . .
It's always the same problem—
Nothing's more abstract, more unreal,
                              than what we actually see.
The job is to make it otherwise.

Two dead crepe-myrtle bushes,
                              tulips petal-splayed and swan-stemmed,
All blossoms gone from the blossoming trees—the new loss
Is not like old loss,
Winter-kill, a jubilant revelation, an artificial thing
Linked and lifted by pure description into the other world.

Self-oblivion, sacred information, God's nudge—
I think I'll piddle around by the lemon tree, thorns
Sharp as angel's teeth.
                              I think
I'll lie down in the dandelions, the purple and white violets.
I think I'll keep on lying there, one eye cocked toward heaven.

April eats from my fingers,
                              nibble of dogwood, nip of pine.
Now is the time, Lord.
Syllables scatter across the new grass, in search of their words.

Such minor Armageddons.
Beside the waters of disremembering,
                    I lay me down.

Star Turn

Nothing is quite as secretive as the way the stars
Take off their bandages and stare out
At the night,
        that dark rehearsal hall,
And whisper their little songs,
The alpha and beta ones, the ones from the great fire.

Nothing is quite as gun shy,
           the invalid, broken pieces
Drifting and rootless, rising and falling, forever
Deeper into the darkness.
Nightly they give us their dumb show, nightly they flash us
Their message and melody,
        frost-sealed, our lidless companions.

A Bad Memory Makes You a Metaphysician,

a Good One Makes You a Saint

This is our world, high privet hedge on two sides,
                                 half-circle of arborvitae,
Small strip of sloped lawn,
Last of the spring tulips and off-purple garlic heads
Snug in the cutting border,
Dwarf orchard down deep at the bottom of things,
                                     God's crucible,
Bat-swoop and grab, grackle yawp, back yard . . .

This is our landscape,
Bourgeois, heartbreakingly suburban;
                                 these are the ashes we rise from.
As night goes down, we watch it darken and disappear.
We push our glasses back on our foreheads,
                              look hard, and it disappears.

In another life, the sun shines and the clouds are motionless.
There, too, the would-be-saints are slipping their hair shirts on.
But only the light souls can be saved;
Only the ones whose weight
                              will not snap the angel's wings.
Too many things are not left unsaid.
If you want what the syllables want, just do your job.

Thinking about the Poet Larry Levis

One Afternoon in Late May

Rainy Saturday, Larry dead
                         almost three weeks now,
Rain starting to pool in the low spots
And creases along the drive.
                         Between showers, the saying goes,
Roses and rhododendron wax glint
Through dogwood and locust leaves,
Flesh-colored, flesh-destined, spring in false flower, goodbye.

The world was born when the devil yawned,
                         the legend goes,
And who's to say it's not true,
Color of flesh, some inner and hidden bloom of flesh.
Rain back again, then back off,
Sunlight suffused like a chest pain across the tree limbs.
God, the gathering night, assumes it.

We haven't a clue as to what counts
In the secret landscape behind the landscape we look at here.
We just don't know what matters,
                         May dull and death-distanced,
Sky half-lit and grackle-ganged—
It's all the same dark, it's all the same absence of dark.
Part of the rain has now fallen, the rest still to fall.

In the Kingdom of the Past,

the Brown-Eyed Man Is King

It's all so pitiful, really, the little photographs
Around the room of places I've been,
And me in them, the half-read books, the fetishes, this
Tiny arithmetic against the dark undazzle.
Who do we think we're kidding?

Certainly not our selves, those hardy perennials
We take such care of, and feed, who keep on keeping on
Each year, their knotty egos like bulbs
Safe in the damp and dreamy soil of their self-regard.
No way we bamboozle them with these

Shrines to the woebegone, ex votos and reliquary sites
One comes in on one's knees to,
The country of *what was*, the country of *what we pretended to be*,
Cruxes and intersections of all we'd thought was fixed.
There is no guilt like the love of guilt.

Passing the Morning under the Serenissima

Noon sun big as a knuckle,
                                    tight over Ponte S. Polo,
Unlike the sighting of Heraclitus the Obscure,
Who said it's the width of a man's foot.
Unable to take the full
                              "clarity" of his fellow man,
He took to the mountains and ate grasses and wild greens,
Aldo Buzzi retells us.

Sick, dropsical, he returned to the city and stretched out on the
           ground
And covered his body with manure
To dry himself out.
                        After two days of cure, he died,
Having lost all semblance of humanity, and was devoured by dogs.
Known as "the weeping philosopher," he said one time,
The living and the dead, the waked and the sleeping, are the same.

Thus do we entertain ourselves on hot days, Aldo Buzzi,
Cees Nooteboom, Gustave Flaubert,
The flies and nameless little insects
                             circling like God's angels
Over the candy dish and worn rug.
The sun, no longer knuckle or foot,
                             strays behind June's flat clouds.
Boats bring their wild greens and bottled water down the
           Republic's shade-splotched canals.

Venetian Dog

Bad day in Bellini country, Venetian dog high-stepper
Out of Carpaccio and down the street,

                              tail like a crozier
Over his ivory back.
A Baron Corvo bad day, you mutter, under your short breath.

Listen, my friend, everything works to our disregard.
Language, our common enemy, moves like the tide against us,
Fortune's heel upwind

                    over Dogana's golden universe
High in the cloud-scratched and distant sky.

Six p.m. Sunday church bells
Flurry and circle and disappear like pigeon flocks,
Lost in the sunlight's fizzle and fall.
The stars move as well against us.

                              From pity, it sometimes seems.

So what's the body to do,

                    caught in its web of spidered flesh?
Venetian dog has figured his out, and stands his ground,
Bristled and hogbacked,
Barking in cadence at something that you and I can't see.

                                                      But

For us, what indeed, lying like S. Lorenzo late at night
On his brazier, lit from above by a hole in the sky,

From below by coals,

                         his arm thrown up,

In Titian's great altarpiece, in supplication, what indeed?

In the Valley of the Magra

In June, above Pontrèmoli, high in the Lunigiana,
The pollen-colored chestnut blooms

                                  sweep like a long cloth
Snapped open over the bunched treetops
And up the mountain as far as the almost-Alpine meadows.
At dusk, in the half-light, they appear
Like stars come through the roots of the great trees from another
      sky.
Or tears, with my glasses off.

                              Sometimes they seem like that
Just as the light fades and the darkness darkens for good.

Or that's the way I remember it when the afternoon
      thunderstorms
Tumble out of the Blue Ridge,
And distant bombardments muscle in

                           across the line
Like God's solitude or God's shadow,
The loose consistency of mortar and river stone
Under my fingers where I leaned out
Over it all,
            isolate farm lights
Starting to take the color on, the way I remember it . . .

Returned to the Yaak Cabin,

I Overhear an Old Greek Song

Back at the west window, Basin Creek
Stumbling its mantra out in a slurred, midsummer monotone,
Sunshine in planes and clean sheets
Over the yarrow and lodgepole pine—
We spend our whole lives in the same place and never leave,
Pine squirrels and butterflies at work in a deep dither,
Bumblebee likewise, wind with a slight hitch in its get-along.

Dead heads on the lilac bush, daisies
Long-legged forest of stalks in a white throw across the field
Above the ford and deer path,
Candor of marble, candor of bone—
We spend our whole lives in the same place and never leave,
The head of Orpheus bobbing in the slatch, his song
Still beckoning from his still-bloody lips, bright as a bee's heart.

Ars Poetica II

I find, after all these years, I am a believer—
I believe what the thunder and lightning have to say;
I believe that dreams are real,

                     and that death has two reprisals;
I believe that dead leaves and black water fill my heart.

I shall die like a cloud, beautiful, white, full of nothingness.

The night sky is an ideogram,

                     a code card punched with holes.
It thinks it's the word of what's-to-come.
It thinks this, but it's only The Library of Last Resort,
The reflected light of The Great Misunderstanding.

God is the fire my feet are held to.

Cicada Blue

I wonder what Spanish poets would say about this,
Bloodless, mid-August meridian,
Afternoon like a sucked-out, transparent insect shell,
Diffused, and tough to the touch.
Something about a labial, probably,

                    something about the blue.

St. John of the Cross, say, or St. Teresa of Avila.
Or even St. Thomas Aquinas,
Who said, according to some,

                "All I have written seems like straw
Compared to what I have seen and what has been revealed to me."
Not Spanish, but close enough,

                    something about the blue.

Blue, I love you, blue, one of them said once in a different color,
The edged and endless
Expanse of nowhere and nothingness

                  hemmed as a handkerchief from here,
Cicada shell of hard light
Just under it, blue, I love you, blue . . .

We've tried to press God in our hearts the way we'd press a leaf
     in a book,
Afternoon memoried now,

                sepia into brown,

Night coming on with its white snails and its ghost of the
     Spanish poet,
Poet of shadows and death.
Let's press him firm in our hearts, O blue, I love you, blue.

All Landscape Is Abstract, and Tends to Repeat Itself

I came to my senses with a pencil in my hand
And a piece of paper in front of me.
                                        To the years
Before the pencil, O, I was the resurrection.
Still, who knows where the soul goes,
Up or down,
                after the light switch is turned off, who knows?

It's late August, and prophets are calling their bears in.

The sacred is frightening to the astral body,
As is its absence.
                    We have to choose which fear is our consolation.
Everything comes *ex alto*,
We'd like to believe, the origin and the end, or
Non-origin and the non-end,
                                each distant and inaccessible.

Over the Blue Ridge, the whisperer starts to whisper in tongues.

Remembered landscapes are left in me
The way a bee leaves its sting,
                                hopelessly, passion-placed,
Untranslatable language.
Non-mystical, insoluble in blood, they act as an opposite
To the absolute, whose words are a solitude, and set to music.

All forms of landscape are autobiographical.

Possum work, world's windowlust, lens of the Byzantine—
Friday in Appalachia.
Hold on, old skeletal life,
                              there's more to come, if I hear right.
Still, even the brightest angel is darkened by time,
Even the sharpest machine
                              dulled and distanced by death.

Wick-end of August, wicked once-weight of summer's sink and
      sigh.

September now, set to set foot on the other side,
Hurricanes sprouting like daisy heads around her lap.
We know where she's been. We know
What big secret she keeps,
                              so dark and dungeoned, and wish her well,
Praying that she will whisper it to us
                              just once, just this once.

The secret of language is the secret of disease.

2

What Do You Write About,

Where Do Your Ideas Come From?

Landscape, of course, the idea of God and language
Itself, that pure grace
                     which is invisible and sure and clear,
Fall equinox two hours old,
Pine cones dangling and doomed over peach tree and privet,
Clouds bulbous and buzzard-traced.
The Big Empty is also a subject of some note,
Dark dark and never again,
The missing word and there you have it,
                             heart and heart beat,
Never again and never again,
Backdrop of back yard and earth and sky
Jury-rigged carefully into place,
Wind from the west and then some,
Everything up and running hard,
                       everything under way,
Never again never again.

Renoir, whose paintings I don't much like,
Says what survives of the artist is the feeling he gives by means
    of objects.
I do like that, however,
The feeling put in as much as the feeling received
To make a work distinctive,
Though I'm not sure it's true,

                     or even it's workable.

—————

When Chekhov died, he died at dawn,

                     a large moth circling the lamp,
Beating its pressed wings.
Placed in a zinc casket, the corpse, labeled *Fresh Oysters*,
Was sent to Moscow in a freight car from Germany.
His last words were, *Has the sailor left?*
I am dying, Ich sterbe.

—————

My breath is corrupt, my days are extinct, the graves are ready for me,
Job says. They change the night into day—
The light is short because of darkness . . .
I have said to corruption,

                 thou art my father, to the worm,
Thou art my mother and my sister—

They shall go down to the bars of the pit,
                                   when our rest together is in the dust.

———————

That's all. There's nothing left after that.
As Meng Chiao says,
                      For a while the dust weighs lightly on my cloak.

Late Saturday afternoon in Charlottesville.

> Columbus Day,

Windless, remorseless Columbus Day,
Sunlight like Scotch tape
Stuck to the surfaces of west-worn magnolia leaves.
Children are playing their silly games
Behind the back yard,

> toneless, bell-less Columbus Day.

Despair's a sweet meat I'd hang a fang in once or twice,
Given the go-ahead.

> And where's October's golden and red,

Where is its puff of white smoke?
Another page torn off

> The Appalachian Book of the Dead,

Indifferent silence of heaven,
Indifferent silence of the world.

Jerusalem, I say quietly, Jerusalem,
The altar of evening starting to spread its black cloth
In the eastern apse of things—
　　the soul that desires to return *home*, desires its own destruction,
We know, which never stopped anyone,
The fear of it and dread of it on every inch of the earth,
Though light's still lovely in the west,

> billowing, purple and scarlet-white.

Indian Summer II

As leaves fall from the trees, the body falls from the soul.
As memory signs transcendence, scales fall from the heart.
As sunlight winds back on its dark spool,
                                        November's a burn and an ache.

A turkey buzzard logs on to the late evening sky.
Residual blood in the oak's veins.
Sunday. Recycling tubs like flower bins at the curb.

Elsewhere, buried up to her armpits,
                                        someone is being stoned to death.
Elsewhere, transcendence searches for us.
Elsewhere, this same story is being retold by someone else.

The heavenly way has been lost,
                                        no use to look at the sky.
Still, the stars, autumnal stars, start to flash and transverberate.
The body falls from the soul, and the soul takes off,
                                        a wandering, moral drug.

This is an end without a story.
This is a little bracelet of flame around your wrist.
This is the serpent in the Garden,
                                        her yellow hair, her yellow hair.

We live in two landscapes, as Augustine might have said,

One that's eternal and divine,

                           and one that's just the back yard,
Dead leaves and dead grass in November, purple in spring.

Autumn's Sidereal, November's a Ball and Chain

After the leaves have fallen, the sky turns blue again,
Blue as a new translation of Longinus on the sublime.
We wink and work back from its edges.
                              We walk around
Under its sequence of metaphors,
Looking immaculately up for the overlooked.
Or looking not so immaculately down for the same thing.

If there's nothing going on, there's no reason to make it up.
Back here, for instance, next to the cankered limbs of the plum
        trees,
We take a load off.
                    Hard frost on the grass blades and wild onion,
Invisibly intricate, so clear.
Pine needles in herringbone, dead lemon leaves, dead dirt.
The metaphysical world is meaningless today,

South wind retelling its autobiography
                              endlessly
Through the white pines, somesuch and susurration, shhh, shhh . . .

Give me the names for things, just give me their real names,
Not what we call them, but what
They call themselves when no one's listening—
At midnight, the moon-plated hemlocks like unstruck bells,
God wandering aimlessly elsewhere.

                                    Their names, their secret names.

December. Everything's black and brown. Or half-black and half-
    brown.
What's still alive puts its arms around me,

                                    amen from the evergreens
That want my heart on their ribbed sleeves.
Why can't I listen to them?

                        Why can't I offer my heart up
To what's in plain sight and short of breath?

Restitution of the divine in a secular circumstance—
Page 10, The Appalachian Book of the Dead,

                                    the dog-eared one,
Pre-solstice winter light laser-beaked, sun over Capricorn,
Dead-leaf-and-ice-mix grunged on the sidewalk and driveway.
Short days. Short days. Dark soon the light overtakes.

                                    Stump of a hand.

Reply to Wang Wei

The dream of reclusive life, a strict, essential solitude,
Is a younger hermit's dream.
Tuesday, five days till winter, a cold, steady rain.
White hair, white heart. The time's upon us and no exit
East of the lotus leaves.
                  No exit, you said, and a cold, steady rain.

Indeed.
        All those walks by the river, all those goodbyes.
Willows shrink back to brown across Locust Avenue,
The mountains are frost and blue
                    and fellow travellers.
Give you peace, you said, freedom from ten thousand matters.
And asked again, does fame come only to the ancients?

At the foot of the southern mountains, white clouds pass without
    end,
You wrote one time in a verse.
                They still do, and still without end.
That's it. Just wanted to let you know it hasn't changed—no out,
    no end,
And fame comes only to the ancients, and justly so,
Rain turning slowly to snow now then back into rain.

Everywhere everywhere, you wrote, something is falling,
The evening mist has no resting place.

31

What time we waste, wasting time.
                              Still, I sit still,
The mind swept clean in its secret shade,
Though no monk from any hill will ever come to call.

Giorgio Morandi and the Talking Eternity Blues

Late April in January, seventy-some-odd degrees.
The entry of Giorgio Morandi in The Appalachian Book of the
    Dead
Begins here, without text, without dates—
A photograph of the master contemplating four of his objects,
His glasses pushed high on his forehead,
                            his gaze replaced and pitiless.

The dove, in summer, coos sixty times a minute, one book says.
Hard to believe that,
                    even in this unseasonable heat,
A couple of them appearing and silent in the bare tree
Above me.
            Giorgio Morandi doesn't blink an eye
As sunlight showers like sulphur grains across his face.

There is an end to language.
                    There is an end to handing out the names of things,
Clouds moving south to north along the Alleghenies
And Blue Ridge, south to north on the wind.
Eternity, unsurprisingly, doesn't give this a take.
Eternity's comfortless, a rock and a hard ground.

Now starless, Madonnaless, Morandi
Seems oddly comforted by the lack of comforting,
A proper thing in its proper place,

Landscape subsumed, language subsumed,

                                    the shadow of God
Liquid and indistinguishable.

Drone and Ostinato

Winter. Cold like a carved thing outside the window glass.
Silence of sunlight and ice dazzle.
$$\text{Stillness of noon.}$$
Dragon back of the Blue Ridge,
Landscape laid open like an old newspaper, memory into
    memory.

Our lives are like birds' lives, flying around, blown away.
We're bandied and bucked on and carried across the sky,
Drowned in the blue of the infinite,
$$\text{blur-white and drift.}$$
We disappear as stars do, soundless, without a trace.

Nevertheless, let's settle and hedge the bet.
$$\text{The wind picks up, clouds cringe,}$$
Snow locks in place on the lawn.
Wordless is what the soul wants, the one thing that I keep in
    mind.
One in one united, bare in bare doth shine.

Ostinato and Drone

The mystic's vision is beyond the world of individuation,
it is beyond speech and thus incommunicable.
— PAUL MENDES-FLOHR, *Ecstatic Confessions*

Undoing the self is a hard road.
Somewhere alongside a tenderness that's infinite,
I gather, and loneliness that's infinite.
                                        No finitude.
There's nothing that bulks up in between.
Radiance. Unending brilliance of light
                          like drops of fire through the world.
Speechless. Incommunicable. At one with the one.

Some dead end—no one to tell it to,
                              nothing to say it with.
That being the case, I'd like to point out this quince bush,
Quiescent and incommunicado in winter shutdown.
I'd like you to notice its long nails
And skeletal underglow.
                        I'd like you to look at its lush
Day-dazzle, noon light and shower shine.

It's reasonable to represent anything that really exists
                            by that thing which doesn't exist,
Daniel Defoe said.
And that's what we're talking about, the difference between the
     voice and the word,
The voice continuing to come back in splendor,
                                    the word still not forthcoming.
We're talking about the bush on fire.
We're talking about this quince bush, its noonday brilliance of light.

"It's Turtles All the Way Down"

I snap the book shut. February. Alternate sky.
Tiny gobbets like pyracantha beans on the mock crab-apple trees.
None of this interests me.

Mercy is made of fire, and fire needs fire, another book says.
It also says, to get to God, pull both your feet back—
One foot from out of this life, one foot from the other.

Outside, I walk off-cadence under the evergreens,
Ground needles bronzed and half mythic, as though from a
    tomb,
5:20 winter lightfall sifted and steeped through medium yellow.

What God is the God behind the God who moves the chess
    pieces,
Borges wondered.
                What mask is the mask behind the mask
The language wears and the landscape wears, I ask myself.

O, well, I let the south wind blow all over my face.
I let the sunshine release me and fall all over my face.
I try not to think of them stopping.

Half February

St. Valentine's. Winter is in us.
Hard to be faithful to summer's bulge and buzz
                                        in such a medicine.
Hard to be heart-wrung
And sappy in what's unworkable and world-weary.
Hard to be halt and half-strung.

All of us, more or less, are unfaithful to something.
Solitude bears us away,
Approaches us in the form of a crescent, like love,
And bears us away
Into its icy comforting, our pain and our happiness.

I saw my soul like a little silkworm, diligently fed,
Spinning a thread with its little snout,
Anna Garcias wrote in the sixteenth century.
And who can doubt her,
Little silkworm in its nonbeing and nothingness.

Nothing like that in these parts these days—
The subject for today, down here, is the verb "to be,"
Snow falling, then sleet, then freezing rain,
St. Catherine nowhere in evidence, her left side opened, her
      heart removed,
All the world's noise, all its hubbub and din,
                                        now chill and a glaze.

Back Yard Boogie Woogie

I look out at the back yard—
                sur le motif, as Paul Cézanne would say,
Nondescript blond winter grass,
Boxwood buzz-cut still dormant with shaved sides, black gum tree
And weeping cherry veined and hived against the afternoon sky.

I try to look at landscape as though I weren't there,
                    but know, wherever I am,
I disturb that place by breathing, by my heart's beating—
I only remember things that I think I've forgot,
Lives the color of dead leaves, for instance, days like dead
    insects.

Most of my life is like that,
                scattered, fallen, overlooked.
Back here, magenta rosettes flock the limbs of the maple trees,
Little thresholds of darkness,
Late February sunlight indifferent as water to all the objects in it.

Only perfection is sufficient, Simone Weil says.
Whew . . .
        Not even mercy or consolation can qualify.
Good thing I've got this early leaf bristle in my hand.
Good thing the cloud shadows keep on keeping on, east-by-
    northeast.

Full moon illuminated large initial for letter M,
Appalachian Book of the Dead, 22 February 1997—
La luna piove, the moon rains down its antibiotic light
Over the sad, septic world,
Hieroglyphs on the lawn, supplicant whispers for the other side,
I am pure, I am pure, I am pure . . .

The soul is in the body as light is in the air,
Plotinus thought.
                    Well, I wouldn't know about that, but
La luna piove, and shines out in every direction—
Under it all, disorder, above,
A handful of stars on one side, a handful on the other.
Whatever afflictions we have, we have them for good.

Such Egyptology in the wind, such raw brushstrokes,
Moon losing a bit from its left side at two o'clock.
Still, light mind-of-Godish,
                    silent deeps where seasons don't exist.
Surely some splendor's set to come forth,
Some last equation solved, declued and reclarified.
South wind and a long shine, a small-time paradiso . . .

Sitting as though suspended from something, cool in my deck
    chair,
Unlooked-on, otherworldly.
There is no acquittal, there is no body of light and elegy.
There is no body of fire.

It is as though an angel had walked across the porch,
A conflagration enhanced, extinguished, then buried again,
No pardon, no nourishment.
It's March, and starvelings feed from my mouth.

Ubi amor, ibi oculus,
                    love sees what the eye sees
Repeatedly, more or less.
It certainly seems so here, the gates of the arborvitae
The gates of mercy look O look they feed from my mouth.

3

Body Language

The human body is not the world, and yet it is.
The world contains it, and is itself contained. Just so.
The distance between the two
Is like the distance between the *no* and the *yes*,
                                abysmal distance,
Nothing and everything. Just so.

This morning I move my body like a spring machine
Among the dormant and semi-dead,
The shorn branches and stubbed twigs
                                hostile after the rain,
Grumpy and tapped out as go-betweens.
Blossoming plum tree coronal toast, cankered and burned.

When body becomes the unbody,
Look hard for its certitude, inclusive, commensurate thing.
Look for its lesson and camouflage.
Look hard for its leash point and linkup.
The shadow of the magnolia tree is short shrift for the grass.

I move through the afternoon,
                          autumnal in pre-spring,
October-headed, hoarfrost-fingered.
The body inside the body is the body I want to come to—
I see it everywhere,
Lisping and licking itself, breaking and entering.

"When You're Lost in Juarez, in the Rain,

and It's Eastertime Too"

Like a grain of sand added to time,
Like an inch of air added to space,
                                    or a half-inch,
We scribble our little sentences.
Some of them sound okay and some of them sound not so okay.
A grain and an inch, a grain and an inch and a half.

Sad word wands, desperate alphabet.

Still, there's been no alternative
Since language fell from the sky.
Though mystics have always said that communication is
        languageless.
And maybe they're right—
                        the soul speaks and the soul receives.
Small room for rebuttal there . . .

Over the Blue Ridge, late March late light annunciatory and
        visitational.

Tonight, the comet Hale-Bopp
                        will ghost up on the dark page of the sky
By its secret juice and design from the full moon's heat.
Tonight, some miracle will happen somewhere, it always does.
Good Friday's a hard rain that won't fall,
Wild onion and clump grass, green on green.

Our mouths are incapable, white violets cover the earth.

High-fiving in Charlottesville.
Sunset heaped up, as close to us as a barrel fire.
Let's all go down to the river,
                    there's a man there that's walking on the water,
On the slow, red Rivanna,
He can make the lame walk, he can make the dumb talk,
                            and open up the eyes of the blind.
That dry-shod, over-the-water walk.

Harbor him in your mind's eye, snub him snug to your hearts.

They'll have to sing louder than that.
                    They'll have to dig deeper into the earbone
For this one to get across.
They'll have to whisper a lot about the radiant body.
Murmur of river run, murmur of women's voices.
Raised up, without rhyme,
                    the murmur of women's voices.
Good luck was all we could think to say.

Dogwood electrified and lit from within by April afternoon late-
    light.

This is the lesson for today—
                    narrative, narrative, narrative . . .
Tomorrow the sun comes back.

Tomorrow the tailings and slush piles will turn to gold
When everyone's down at the river.
The muscadines will bring forth,
The mountain laurel and jack-in-heaven,
                                    while everyone's down at the river.

Spring Storm

After the rainfall, a little Buddha in each water drop,
After the rainfall, a little rainbow in each one,
Sun like a one-eyed, Venetian Doge
                                checking it out,
Then letting the clouds slide shut.
The Chinese can guide you to many things,
                                but the other side's not one of them,
Water reflecting sun's fire, then not.

And the stars keep on moving—
                                no one can tie them to one place.
Doge eye from under the cloud, sky mullioned with oak limbs,
Stars moving unseen behind the light surge, great river.
The end of desire is the beginning of wisdom,
We keep on telling ourselves,
                                lone crow
In sun-splotch now crawling across the lawn, black on black.

Early Saturday Afternoon, Early Evening

Saturday. Early afternoon. High
Spring light through new green,
                              a language, it seems, I have forgotten,
But which I'll remember soon enough
When the first pages are turned
                              in The Appalachian Book of the Dead.
The empty ones. The ones about the shining and stuff.

Father darkness, mother abyss,
                              the shadow whispered,
Abolish me, make me light.
And so it happened. Rumor of luminous bodies.
The face on the face of the water became no face.
The words on the page of the book became a hush.
                              And luminous too.

These things will come known to you,
                              these things make soft your shift,
Alliteration of lost light, aspirate hither-and-puff,
Afternoon undervoices starting to gather and lift off
In the dusk,
              Red Rover, Red Rover, let Billy come over,
Laughter and little squeals, a quick cry.

"The Holy Ghost Asketh for Us with Mourning

and Weeping Unspeakable"

Well, sainthood's a bottomless pity,

                                   as some wag once said, so

Better forget about that.

I'd rather, in any case, just sit here and watch the rose bleed.

I'd rather it it than me.

For that's how the world proceeds, I've found out,

                                   some blood and a lot of *watch*.

Still, I like to think of them there in their gold gowns and hair
    shirts,

Missing whatever was lost or lopped

Their last time around,

                                 its absence revealing a pride of place.

I like to think of their tender flesh

Just healed, or just beginning to heal,

                                 syrupy, sweet like that.

Whatever has been will be again,

                               unaltered, ever-returning.

Serenity of the rhododendron, pink and white,

Dark cinnamon, pink and white,

Azaleas opening in their own deep sleep. Ours too.

After-rupture of tulip border, and

                            white light in the green.

Unseen, unlistened to, unspoken of.

                       Salvation.

Light is, light is not, light is—
However you look at it, the heaven of the contemplatives is a
   hard gig.
Thrones and Dominions they'd drift among.
The landscape and wild chestnut will not remember them.

Half-asleep on the back deck,

                    low wasp-hum of power mower

Ebbing and coming back from next door,

Aggressive shadows of maple leaves

                    crabbing across the shy sunlight

Languishing apprehensively over the fresh-stained pine boards.

Half-silence, 5 p.m. traffic tide, half-silence, violin tone scales.

So, where do we go from here,

Indoors now, great rush of wheels in my head, it is spring—

Vacancy, earth life, remains out there,

                    somewhere in the machine.

Waiting for something to come—anything—and mushroom,

I think of myself as a hare, as Virginia Woolf once said,

                    stilled, expecting moon-visitors.

When your answers have satisfied the forty-two gods,

When your heart's in balance with the weight of a feather,

When your soul is released like a sibyl from its cage,

Like a wind you'll cross over,

                    not knowing how, not knowing where,

Remembering nothing, unhappening, hand and foot.

The world's a glint on the window glass,

The landscape's a flash and fall,

                    sudden May rain like a sleet spill

On the tin roof, no angel, night dark.
Eternity puddles up.
And here's the Overseer, blue, and O he is blue . . .

Star Turn II

How small the stars are tonight, bandannaed by moonlight,
How few and how far between—
Disordered and drained, like highlights in Dante's death mask.
Or a sequined dress from the forties

                            —hubba-hubba—
Some sequins missing, some sequins inalterably in place.

Unlike our lives, which are as they are.
Unlike our imagined selves, which are as we'll never become,
Star-like and shining,
Everyone looking up at, everyone pointing there, O there,
Masked and summering in,

           each one a bright point, each one a dodged eclipse.

After Reading T'ao Ch'ing, I Wander Untethered

Through the Short Grass

Dry spring, no rain for five weeks.
Already the lush green begins to bow its head and sink to its
    knees.

Already the plucked stalks and thyroid weeds like insects
Fly up and trouble my line of sight.

I stand inside the word *here*
                    as that word stands in its sentence,
Unshadowy, half at ease.

Religion's been in a ruin for over a thousand years.
Why shouldn't the sky be tatters,
                      lost notes to forgotten songs?

I inhabit who I am, as T'ao Ch'ing says, and walk about
Under the mindless clouds.
                    When it ends, it ends. What else?

One morning I'll leave home and never find my way back—
My story and I will disappear together, just like this.

Remembering Spello, Sitting Outside in

Prampolini's Garden

In and out of the shy, limp leaves of the grape arbor,
Song birds slither and peel back.

High in the Umbrian sky, the ghosts
Of true saints pinwheel and congregate like pale, afternoon
        clouds
Ready to jump-start the universe,

The Gates of Propertius—so they say—
                        cream-porphyry at the west of town,
Monte Subasio north-northwest.

It's getting late. The white dog has buried her bits of bread and
The early apricots start to shine,
                        forty-watt bulbs
Against the sundowned and mottled plain.

No word for time, no word for God, landscape exists outside
        each,
But stays, incurable ache, both things,

And bears me out as evening darkens and steps forth,
                        my body snug in my life
As a gun in its carrying case,
As an old language, an old address.

I sit in my plastic lawn chair,

                    unearthly and dispossessed,

My eyes on the turning stars.

Like a Roman statue, I watch everything and see nothing.

Just under the surface of the earth,

The traffic continues to glide by

                        all night with its lights off.

After Rereading Robert Graves, I Go Outside

to Get My Head Together

Fourth of July. A stillness across the morning like
The inside of the inside of a hot, uncomforting place.
Head-hunting sky, high clouds lingering, half-suggestive,
Mare's-tailed and double layered.
Green leaves. Clouds and sky. Green leaves. Clouds. Sky.

According to Graves, the true function of poetry
Is a strict, religious invocation of the Muse.
Tell it to the Marines, Roberto,
                                    the Muse is as dead as God is.
In memory of the Muse, perhaps—
In memory of a Memory: a hidden face, a long, white veil.

And yet The Appalachian Book of the Dead exists,
In part, to ease an exit, praise the present and praise the past,
To click the abacus beads, to sum their cloudy count.   ˙
(Though sometimes subtraction seems the thing,
A little less of this, a little less of all that.)

Early summer, idle images. No wind, no wound,
The world unpetaled and opened to anyone's tongue.
My next-door neighbor's lawn sprinkler crests and collapses
    beyond the hedge,
A cardinal taunts me from her branch.
                                    Now bees drag their wet loads
Across the garden to feed their queen, huge in her humming hive.

American Twilight

Why do I love the sound of children's voices in unknown games
So much on a summer's night,
Lightning bugs lifting heavily out of the dry grass
Like alien spacecraft looking for higher ground,
Darkness beginning to sift like coffee grains

over the neighborhood?

Whunk of a ball being kicked,
Surf-suck and surf-spill from traffic along the bypass,
American twilight,

Venus just lit in the third heaven,
Time-tick between "Okay, let's go," and "This earth is not my
home."

Why do I care about this? Whatever happens will happen
With or without us,

with or without these verbal amulets.
In the first ply, in the heaven of the moon, a little light,
Half-light, over Charlottesville.
Trees reshape themselves, the swallows disappear, lawn sprinklers
do the wave.

Nevertheless, it's still summer: cicadas pump their boxes,
Jack Russell terriers, as they say, start barking their heads off,
And someone, somewhere, is putting his first foot, then the second,
Down on the other side,

no hand to help him, no tongue to wedge its weal.

Last page, The Appalachian Book of the Dead,
full moon,
No one in anyone's arms, no lip to ear, cloud bank
And boyish soprano out of the east edge of things.
Ball-whomp and rig-grind stage right,
Expectancy, quivering needle, at north-northwest.

And here comes the angel with her drum and wings. Some
wings.
Lost days, as Meng Chiao says, a little window of words
We peer through darkly. Darkly,
Moon stopped in cloud bank, light slick for the chute and long
slide,
No lip, no ear.
Distant murmur of women's voices.

I hear that the verb is facilitate. To facilitate.
Azure. To rise. To rise through the azure. Illegible joy.
No second heaven. No first.
I think I'll lie here like this awhile, my back flat on the floor.
I hear that days bleed.
I hear that the right word will take your breath away.

Landscape as Metaphor,

Landscape as Fate and a Happy Life

August. Montana. The black notebook open again.
Across the blue-veined, dune-flattened, intimate blank of the page,
An almost-unseeable winged insect has set forth
On foot.
        I think I'll track his white trail.

—To set one's mind on the ink-line, to set one's heart on the dark
Unknowable, is far and forlorn, wouldn't you say?

Up here, our lives continue to lift off like leaf spores in the
      noon-wash,
Spruce trees and young hemlocks stand guard like Egyptian dogs
At the mouth of the meadow,
Butterflies flock like angels,
               and God knees our necks to the ground.

—Nevertheless, the stars at midnight blow in the wind like high
      cotton.
There is no place in the world they don't approach and pass over.

Wind lull, midmorning, tonight's sky
                      light-shielded, monkish and grand
Behind the glare's iconostasis, yellow poppies

Like lip prints against the log wall, the dead sister's lunar words
Like lip prints against it, this is as far as it goes . . .

—The sun doesn't shine on the same dog's back every day.
Only you, Fragrant One, are worthy to judge us and move on.

Mid-August meltdown, Assurbanipal in the west,
Scorched cloud-towers, crumbling thrones—
The ancients knew to expect a balance at the end of things,
The burning heart against the burning feather of truth.
                                        Sweet-mouthed,
Big ibis-eyed, in the maple's hieroglyphs, I write it down.

All my life I've looked for this slow light, this smallish light
Starting to seep, coppery blue,
                    out of the upper right-hand corner of things,
Down through the trees and off the back yard,
Rising and falling at the same time, now rising, now falling,
Inside the lapis lazuli of late afternoon.

Until the clouds stop, and hush.
Until the left hedge and the right hedge,
                                the insects and short dogs,
The back porch and barn swallows grain-out and disappear.
Until the bypass is blown with silence, until the grass grieves.
Until there is nothing else.

Notes

"Stray Paragraphs in April, Year of the Rat." Simone Weil's notebooks.

"A Bad Memory Makes You a Metaphysician, a Good One Makes You a Saint." The title as well as two lines in the text have been taken and laundered from material in E. M. Cioran's *Tears and Saints*, translated by Ilinca Zarifopol-Johnston, 1995.

"In the Valley of the Magra." Gerard Manley Hopkins, *The Poems of Gerard Manley Hopkins*, 4th edition, "In the Valley of the Elwy," 1970.

"All Landscape Is Abstract, and Tends to Repeat Itself." Guido Ceronetti, *The Silence of the Body*, translated by Michael Moore, 1993.

"Autumn's Sidereal, November's a Ball and Chain." Wallace Stevens, "Jonga," *Collected Poems of Wallace Stevens*, 1965.

"Reply to Wang Wei." *Poems of Wang Wei*, translated by G. W. Robinson, 1973.

"Drone and Ostinato." *Ecstatic Confessions* (Meister Eckhart), compiled by Martin Buber, edited by Paul Mendes-Flohr, 1985.

"Ostinato and Drone." Ibid.

"Half February." Ibid. Thomas Merton/Czeslaw Milosz, *Striving Towards Being*, edited by Robert Faggen, 1997.

"Back Yard Boogie Woogie." Simone Weil, *Waiting for God*, translated by Emma Craufurd, 1973.

"Opus Posthumous II." Ezra Pound, "Canto 90," *The Cantos*, 1970.

"When You're Lost in Juarez, in the Rain, and It's Eastertime Too" (sic). Bob Dylan; I. M. Pei.

"The Appalachian Book of the Dead IV." Mac Wiseman, "Let's All Go Down to the River" (trad.).

"Spring Storm." Gary Snyder, *Mountains and Rivers Without End*, 1996.

"The Appalachian Book of the Dead V." *The Diaries of Virginia Woolf.*

"After Reading T'ao Ch'ing . . ." *The Selected Poems of T'ao Ch'ing*, translated by David Hinton.